BEER

for Breakfast

ISBN-13: 978-1-56383-595-7
Item #7155

Printed in the USA

Distributed By:

507 Industrial Street
Waverly, IA 50677

www.cqbookstore.com

gifts@cqbookstore.com

 CQ Products

 CQ Products

 @cqproducts

 @cqproducts

Beer for Breakfast?

Let's face it, getting out of bed in the morning is a little easier knowing a scrumptious breakfast is waiting for you... and think how fast you'd hop out of bed if that breakfast involved beer.

Now, you may be wondering if it's okay to have beer for breakfast. Let me be the first to tell you, it is very okay. In fact, up until a couple hundred years ago, beer was the breakfast drink of choice. Granted, this was mostly because plain water was often contaminated, but hey – better safe than sorry, right?

Luckily, there are plenty of ways to honor the age-old tradition of breakfast beers. Not only can you sip a beer alongside your breakfast, but you can make a yummy morning cocktail or use it as the star ingredient in your food. Any way you pour it, there's bound to be a little something for everyone.

Beer Stack

5 eggs
2 C. pancake mix
2 T. sugar
½ tsp. cinnamon
2 T. melted butter

½ C. **lager**
  (*we used orange flavored*)
Butter and maple syrup
  for serving

Directions

Crack the eggs into a big bowl. Grab a whisk and beat them like crazy. Dump in the pancake mix, sugar, and cinnamon. Stir in the butter and beer. Only stir until everything is combined – you want it to have some lumps and bumps.

Heat a griddle and spritz it with nonstick spray. Using about ⅓ cup of batter for each pancake, pour the batter onto the griddle and cook until golden brown on both sides, flipping once with a big spatula.

Stack 'em up, throw on a pat of butter, and drizzle with maple syrup.

Beer is truly the secret ingredient in these pancakes. The carbonation acts like a leavening agent and makes the pancakes extra thick and fluffy.

Stack 'em high and raise your glasses – it's time for breakfast!

Beer popsicles? What is this world coming to? Lotsa fun, that's what!

Pucker Pops

½ C. mandarin oranges, peeled
½ C. fresh raspberries
1 C. vanilla Greek yogurt
¼ C. milk
2 tsp. honey
¼ C. **grapefruit beer**
½ C. granola

Directions

Dump the mandarin oranges and raspberries into a food processor and let it rip until you have small chunks of fruit; dump the fruit into a medium bowl. Stir in the yogurt, milk, honey, and grapefruit beer until well blended. Stir in the granola.

Divide the yogurt mixture evenly among popsicle molds and set them upright *(not fall-down-drunk horizontal)* in the freezer for several hours. Preferably overnight.

In the morning, when you're stumbling to the kitchen looking for something to eat, all you need to do is pull one out of the freezer and prepare to get your brain freeze on.

Makes about 10

This is a grown-up version of your favorite childhood breakfast (or current breakfast – who's judging?).

Lemon Breakfast Tarts

Preheat the oven to 400° and line a baking sheet with parchment paper. Flour a work surface and unroll 4 (9") pre-made pie crusts. Cut off the rounded edges and discard; cut each crust square into 6 rectangles.

Beat together 1 egg and 1 T. **wheat beer** and set aside.

For the filling, whisk together 1 C. fresh lemon juice, zest of 1 lemon, ½ C. **wheat beer**, ½ C. sugar, 2 T. cornstarch, ½ C. melted butter, 2 whole eggs, and 6 yolks until combined. Pour into a saucepan over medium heat and stir until thickened, about 10 minutes. Spoon 2 T. filling into the center of 12 crusts; brush the edges with egg wash and top with the remaining crusts. Seal the edges with a fork and brush the tops with egg wash; bake for 15 to 18 minutes. For the glaze, whisk together 1 C. powdered sugar, 3 T. beer, and 1 tsp. lemon zest. Drizzle on the tarts and enjoy!

Make these the night before and you'll wake up to all the breakfast essentials packed into a hot little biscuit... now that's thinking ahead.

Hot Little Breakfast Biscuits

2 C. flour, plus more for dusting
2 tsp. baking powder
¼ tsp. baking soda

1 T. sugar
1 tsp. salt

continued next page

1 tsp. coarse-ground black pepper
¼ tsp. garlic powder
¼ C. chopped chives
1 C. **hefeweizen**
½ C. chopped deli ham
½ C. shredded cheddar cheese
6 T. melted butter, divided

Directions

Whisk together 2 cups flour, baking powder, baking soda, sugar, salt, black pepper, garlic powder, and chives until well mixed. Add the beer, ham, cheese, and 5 tablespoons melted butter. Stir together until just combined and turn out onto a floured surface.

Roll the dough into a ½"-thick circle. Cut out biscuits with a round biscuit cutter and place on a greased baking sheet. Bake for 20 minutes. Remove from the oven and brush the tops with the remaining 1 tablespoon melted butter. Place back in the oven for 5 minutes more. Serve with Garlic Chive Butter.

Garlic Chive Butter
*With an electric mixer, beat together 1 C. softened butter, 2 T. **hefeweizen**, ½ tsp. minced garlic, ½ tsp. salt, 1 tsp. coarse-ground black pepper, and ¼ C. chopped chives. Cover and chill for at least 1 hour to let the flavors meld.*

9

C'mon sleepyhead – this is the easiest breakfast in the world. Make the spreads ahead of time so you can get up in the morning and just eat.

Bagel Toppers

PB & Chocolate Mix 3 T. peanut butter, 1 T. softened cream cheese, and a healthy splash of a **chocolate porter**; spread onto a cinnamon-raisin bagel and top with crushed peanuts.

Deli Style Mix 3 oz. softened cream cheese with a splash of your favorite **lager**, 1½ tsp. sour cream, some green onion, and a pinch each of garlic powder and salt; smear onto an everything bagel. Top with deli roast beef.

Onion & Lox Mix 3 oz. softened cream cheese with some chopped red onion. Stir in a bit of **hefeweizen** and schmear onto an onion bagel. Top with smoked salmon and a few capers if you have some in your fridge.

Pork & Apple Meatballs

1 egg
½ C. quick-cooking oats
½ C. grated Gala apple
½ tsp. dried parsley
½ tsp. salt
¼ tsp. black pepper
1 lb. ground pork breakfast sausage
¼ C. apple butter
¼ C. pure maple syrup
¼ C. **brown ale**

Directions

Preheat the oven to 400°.
Line a 9 x 13" baking dish with foil; coat with nonstick spray and set aside. In a large bowl, beat the egg lightly with a fork. Stir in the oats, apple, parsley, salt, and pepper. Add the sausage and mix until combined. Shape the mixture into 12 meatballs and place in the prepared baking dish. Bake for 12 to 15 minutes or until cooked through.

In a small saucepan, heat the apple butter, maple syrup, and beer over medium heat, whisking until it begins to bubble. Brush half of the glaze over the baked meatballs and bake 3 minutes more. Remove from the oven and brush with the remaining glaze.

Shhh... this is basically a giant sugar cookie, but since it's covered in fruit, no one will suspect a thing.

Brewer's Fruit Pizza

¾ C. softened butter
¾ C. granulated sugar
¾ C. brown sugar, divided
1 egg yolk
⅓ C. plus 1 T. **brown ale**, divided

1½ tsp. vanilla, divided
1¼ C. all-purpose flour
1 C. bread flour
1¼ tsp. baking soda
1 tsp. baking powder

continued next page

½ tsp. salt
1 tsp. cornstarch
8 oz. cream cheese, softened
Fresh fruit

Directions

Preheat oven to 325°. Grease a 13" pizza pan with nonstick spray and set aside.

In a stand mixer, cream together the butter, granulated sugar, and ½ cup brown sugar. Add the egg yolk, ⅓ cup beer, and ½ teaspoon vanilla and mix until combined. Mix in both types of flour, baking soda, baking powder, salt, and cornstarch. Press the dough into the pizza pan. Bake for 13 to 15 minutes and set aside to cool.

For the frosting, beat the cream cheese with the remaining ¼ cup brown sugar, remaining 1 teaspoon vanilla, and the remaining 1 tablespoon beer. Spread on the cooled crust and top with your favorite fruit.

Fizzy Navel
*A splash of beer adds a little fizz to this classic cocktail. Pour ½ oz. vodka, 1 oz. peach schnapps, 6 oz. **light lager**, and 4 oz. orange juice into a large glass. Stir to combine and add ice to fill.* **Makes 1**

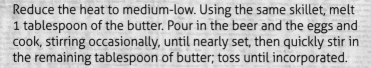

Rise & Shine Morning Tacos

4 small flour tortillas
2 T. butter, divided
2 T. **Belgian wheat beer**
4 eggs, lightly beaten
1 avocado, thinly sliced

¼ C. sliced cherry tomatoes
1 green onion, thinly sliced
¼ C. chopped fresh cilantro
¼ C. hot sauce
¼ C. crumbled Cotija cheese

Directions

Heat a big skillet over medium-high heat. One at a time, heat the tortillas until lightly charred in places; set aside.

Reduce the heat to medium-low. Using the same skillet, melt 1 tablespoon of the butter. Pour in the beer and the eggs and cook, stirring occasionally, until nearly set, then quickly stir in the remaining tablespoon of butter; toss until incorporated.

On each of the charred tortillas, layer avocado, cooked eggs, tomatoes, green onion, cilantro, hot sauce, and cheese. Pour a nice tall glass of beer and enjoy your breakfast.

These breakfast tacos bring the heat. They'd pair well with a lager, IPA, or amber ale. You may want to try all three so you know which is best. You know... for science.

There's very little beer in these tacos. BUT the recipe is absolutely delicious and tastes so perfect along with an ice-cold beer, that drinking one simply must be part of the meal.

Make this bread ahead of time and whip it out at breakfast time. Your hungry, and perhaps hungover, friends will thank you.

Blueberry-Lemon Beer Bread

2 C. plus 1 T. flour, divided
2 T. baking powder
1 tsp. baking soda
½ tsp. salt
¾ C. sugar
¼ C. coconut oil, room temp
2 T. unsweetened applesauce

1 tsp. vanilla
Zest of 1 lemon
⅔ C. **blueberry ale**
5 T. fresh lemon juice, divided
1 C. fresh blueberries
1 C. powdered sugar

Directions

Preheat the oven to 350°
and grease a 5 x 9" loaf pan.

In a medium bowl, whisk together 2 cups flour, baking powder, baking soda, and salt; set aside.

In a big mixing bowl, cream together the sugar and oil. Add the applesauce, vanilla, and zest; mix until combined. In a 1-cup measuring cup, combine the beer and 3 tablespoons lemon juice. Alternately add the dry ingredients and the beer mixture to the applesauce mixture, beating until just combined.

In a separate bowl, mix the blueberries with the remaining 1 tablespoon flour *(this helps keep the blueberries from sinking to the bottom of the bread)*. Fold the blueberries into the batter and pour into the loaf pan. Bake for 50 minutes or until a toothpick inserted into the center comes out clean.

Let the bread cool for 15 minutes, then carefully remove it from the pan and let cool completely.

Once the bread is cool, stir together the powdered sugar and the remaining 2 tablespoons lemon juice. Drizzle the glaze over the cooled bread.

Cherry Punch
Mix 12 oz. tart cherry juice, 6 oz. light rum, 2½ oz. cherry liqueur, and 2 oz. fresh lime juice. Refrigerate at least 2 hours or overnight. When you're ready to serve it, transfer the mixture to a big pitcher and add 16 oz. **sour beer**. *Drink immediately to take advantage of all those suds!* **Serves 4**

Some consider chai tea to be a healthy alternative to coffee... the jury's still out on how healthy this version is, but if it makes you happy, it can't be that bad. Right? Right.

Chai Beer Latte

In a small saucepan, bring 1 C. water and 1 C. **vanilla porter** to a boil. Remove from heat and add 3 chai tea bags; let steep for 6 minutes *(or longer if you want to ramp up the chai flavor)*. Remove the tea bags and bring the tea to a simmer over medium-low heat. Whisk in 2 C. milk, ¼ C. heavy cream, ½ C. brown sugar, and ½ tsp. vanilla. Let simmer until the brown sugar dissolves. Serve topped with a big ol' dollop of whipped cream and a dash of cinnamon. Now that's a latte to get out of bed for.

Bacon & Beer Waffles

Makes about 6

4 eggs
¾ C. **hefeweizen**
¼ C. melted butter
2 T. maple syrup
¼ C. buttermilk
¼ C. plus 2 T. sugar, divided
½ tsp. salt
2 C. flour
1 tsp. cornstarch
½ tsp. baking soda
6 crisp-cooked bacon strips, divided
Butter and syrup for serving

Directions

Separate the eggs. Place the yolks in a bowl and add the beer, butter, syrup, buttermilk, and ¼ cup sugar; whisk until combined. Place the whites in a separate bowl; add the salt and whip with a hand mixer until stiff peaks form. Beat in the remaining 2 tablespoons sugar until well combined.

In a large bowl, combine the flour, cornstarch, baking soda, and 4 crumbled bacon strips. Add the egg mixture to the dry ingredients; stir until just combined and gently fold in the egg whites. Preheat the waffle iron and cook the waffles according to manufacturer instructions. Serve topped with the remaining crumbled bacon, butter, and a drizzle of syrup.

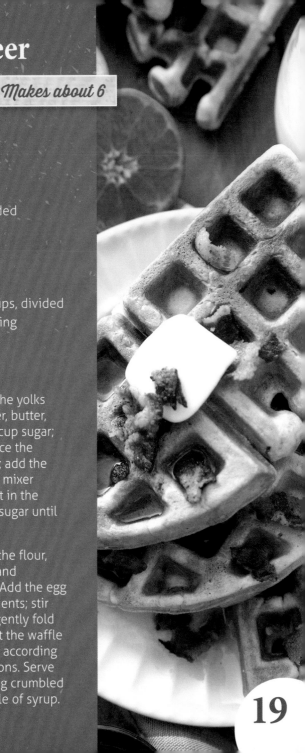

19

Strawberry and rhubarb – just like the muffins Grandma used to make. NOT! (Unless, of course, she was an awesome beer-sluggin' granny. Then good for her!)

Straw-Beery Rhubarb Muffins

2 C. sliced rhubarb *(fresh or frozen & thawed)*

1⅓ C. **strawberry flavored beer**, divided

1¼ C. brown sugar, divided

½ C. old-fashioned oats

½ tsp. cinnamon

2 T. plus ¼ C. melted unsalted butter, divided

1¾ C. flour

2 tsp. baking powder

¾ tsp. salt

2 eggs

Directions

Preheat the oven to 400° and line 12 muffin tins with foil liners.

Grab a medium saucepan. Toss in the rhubarb and add ⅓ cup beer and ¼ cup brown sugar. Cook on high until it boils, then reduce the heat and simmer until it thickens, about 10 minutes. There's a little beer left – you should probably sip on it while you're waiting.

In a bowl, mix the oats, cinnamon, ½ cup brown sugar, and 2 tablespoons butter. Set aside. This is the streusel topping.

Now, grab a big bowl and dump in the flour, baking powder, and salt. In a separate bowl, whisk together the eggs, vanilla, remaining 1 cup beer, remaining ½ cup brown sugar, and remaining ¼ cup butter. Stir the wet ingredients into the dry ingredients until just barely mixed. Add the rhubarb mixture and give it a quick stir.

Divide the batter evenly among the muffin liners and top with streusel. Bake for 20 to 25 minutes, until a toothpick comes out clean. Ta-Dah!

Early Bird Bellini
Pit, peel, and blend 4 ripe peaches; pour through a fine mesh strainer and refrigerate until cold. Add 1 oz. peach purée to a glass and top with **light beer.** *Now that's classy.* **Makes 1**

Beer Brat Hash

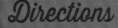

3 Yukon gold potatoes, diced
1 small white onion, diced
1 red bell pepper, diced
12 oz. **pilsner**
1 T. olive oil
1 C. frozen corn
4 brats, casings removed
½ tsp. black pepper
1 tsp. salt
½ tsp. garlic salt
½ C. shredded cheddar cheese

Directions

Throw the potatoes, onion, and pepper into a bowl; pour in the beer and toss to coat. Let chill in the fridge for 30 minutes.

Heat the oil in a large skillet over medium-high heat. Reserve ¼ cup beer from the potatoes and drain the rest. Add the potato mixture to the skillet along with the corn and brats; break the brats into smaller pieces as they cook. Season with black pepper, salt, and garlic salt. Once the meat is almost cooked, add the reserved beer; continue cooking until the meat is cooked, potatoes are tender, and the beer has evaporated. Top with cheese and enjoy!

Serves 4

Beer-glazed bacon – how can it be anything but fantastic?? Bonus: the kitchen smells like pure bliss! Yes, bliss!

Honey-Maple Pig Tails

Preheat the oven to 350° and line a rimmed baking sheet with aluminum foil. Arrange 8 thick-cut bacon strips on the foil and bake for about 20 minutes. In the meantime, combine ¼ C. honey and ¼ C. pure maple syrup in a saucepan; bring to a boil over medium heat. Reduce the heat and simmer for 3 to 4 minutes. Stir in ½ C. **dark lager** and simmer until reduced by half. Remove the pan from the heat and whisk in 1½ tsp. grainy mustard and 1½ tsp. dry mustard. Blot the bacon with paper towels to remove extra grease *(too much grease – blech)* and brush the glaze over the top of the bacon. Reduce the oven temp to 300° and bake about 40 minutes, until crispy-chewy; drain on paper towels, keeping the glazed side up. Enjoy immediately!

Be warned... this behemoth isn't your typical fruit-filled breakfast braid. Don't get your hopes up for any leftovers.

Breakfast Braid of Champions

¾ lb. ground breakfast sausage
1 small yellow onion, chopped
½ C. chopped white button mushrooms
1 garlic clove, minced

¼ tsp. salt
¼ tsp. black pepper
¾ C. **brown ale**, divided
4 oz. cream cheese
2 green onions, sliced

continued next page

2 T. chopped fresh parsley
1 (8 oz.) tube refrigerated crescent rolls
½ C. shredded Pepper Jack cheese
1 egg, lightly beaten

Directions

Preheat oven to 350°.

In a skillet over medium heat, sauté the sausage, onion, mushrooms, garlic, salt, and black pepper until the sausage is almost cooked through. Add ½ cup beer and simmer for 8 minutes; drain the excess liquid. Add the cream cheese, green onions, and parsley; cook over low heat until the cheese is melted.

Unroll the crescent dough onto a greased baking sheet. Roll into a 10 x 12" rectangle, pressing the perforations to seal shut. Spoon the sausage mixture lengthwise down the center of the dough; sprinkle with Pepper Jack cheese. Along each long side of the dough, cut 1" wide stripes 3" into the center. Starting at one end, fold alternating strips at an angle across the filling. Whisk together the egg and the remaining ¼ cup beer. Seal the ends shut and brush with the egg mixture. Bake for 25 minutes or until golden brown.

Grapefruit Radler
Grab a big ol' glass and combine 4 oz. grapefruit juice, 2 oz. pineapple juice, and 6 oz. **wheat beer**. Add ice to fill. You'll be bright eyed and bushy tailed in no time. Makes 1

What could possibly make scones taste even better? Beer. The answer is always beer. Try pairing one of these scones with a hot cup o' joe or a cold winter ale.

Cranberry & Ale
SCONES

5 C. flour
2 T. baking powder
1½ tsp. salt
½ C. sugar
2 C. heavy cream

½ C. dried cranberries
1¼ C. **winter ale**, divided
2 C. powdered sugar
1 tsp. vanilla

Directions

Preheat an oven to 375° and line a rimmed baking sheet with parchment paper.

In a big bowl, combine flour, baking powder, salt, and sugar. Stir in the cream, cranberries, and 1 cup of the beer until just moistened (*do not overmix or thou shalt be rewarded with tough hockey pucks instead of perfect scones*).

Turn the dough onto a lightly floured surface and knead briefly. Divide the dough in half and roll each to a ½"-thick circle. Cut six wedges from each circle and set them all on the prepped baking sheet; bake for 25 to 30 minutes, until golden and delicious-looking. Remove the scones from the pan and set aside for 10 minutes.

In the meantime, make the icing by stirring together the powdered sugar, vanilla, and the remaining ¼ cup beer until smooth. Drizzle over the scones.

The electrolytes in coconut water are believed to fight off a hangover. This cocktail uses cream of coconut instead. That's close enough, right?

Coffee & Cream

½ oz. coffee liqueur
1 oz. cream of coconut
1 oz. heavy cream
1½ oz. dark rum
2 oz. **chocolate porter**
½ oz. allspice dram*
Dash of angostura bitters

Directions

Shake the coffee liqueur, cream of coconut, heavy cream, rum, porter, allspice dram, and angostura bitters in a cocktail shaker filled with ice. Strain into a rocks glass filled with ice. Garnish with a dash of cinnamon.

* If you can't find allspice dram, make it by steeping 3 T. whole allspice (lightly crushed) and 1 crushed cinnamon stick in ½ C. light rum. Shake well and let steep for 7 days, then strain the liquid through a fine mesh strainer. Heat 1 C. water and ½ C. brown sugar, stirring to dissolve. Let the syrup cool and add it to the allspice infusion.

Makes 1

Some believe coffee stout to be the most breakfast-y beer out there (because... it's COFFEE), so why not soak some French toast in it?

Double Brewed French Toast

In a big bowl, whisk together 5 eggs, ½ C. milk, 1 C. **coffee stout**, 1 T. vanilla, and cinnamon to taste. Cut 1 loaf Italian bread into 1"-thick slices and soak in the egg mixture, making sure both sides are well coated. Melt 2 T. butter in a big skillet over medium heat. Add the soaked bread to the skillet and toast until both sides are deep golden brown. To serve, spread each slice with softened cream cheese and drizzle with maple syrup.

Coffee and stout share common flavor characteristics that make them perfect compliments to each other. If you're a coffee drinker, chances are you'll be a fan of stouts.

This will keep you full and give you a good base, just in case breakfast is just the beginning of your beer-filled day. As they say, preparedness is key.

Sausage & Kale Frittata

12 oz. **lager**, divided

2 medium Yukon gold potatoes, cubed

1 T. olive oil

½ lb. pork breakfast sausage

1 white onion, diced

½ lb. mushrooms, sliced

1 C. kale

6 eggs, lightly beaten

¼ C. sour cream

¼ tsp. salt

½ tsp. black pepper

¼ tsp. garlic salt

1 C. shredded cheddar cheese, divided

Salsa for serving

Directions

Preheat the oven to 350°. Fill a pot halfway with water and add 6 ounces beer; boil the potatoes until tender.

Heat the oil in a medium oven-proof skillet over medium heat and cook the sausage, onion, and mushrooms until the sausage is almost cooked through. Add the remaining beer and cook until the sausage is no longer pink and most of the beer has evaporated. Drain the potatoes and add to the skillet along with the kale; cook until the kale wilts.

Meanwhile, whisk together the eggs, sour cream, salt, black pepper, garlic salt, and ½ cup cheese. Pour the eggs on top of the sausage mixture; cook for 3 minutes more. Sprinkle with the remaining ½ cup cheese and place in the oven until the cheese is bubbly and golden brown, about 5 minutes. Serve with salsa.

Wake Me Up Salsa

*Remove the stems and seeds from 2 jalapeños and 1 yellow bell pepper; roughly chop and add to a food processor along with 6 roughly chopped Roma tomatoes, ½ C. chopped red onion, 1 garlic clove, ½ tsp. salt, ½ tsp. black pepper, and a handful of chopped fresh cilantro; process until coarsely chopped. Drain the excess liquid through a fine mesh strainer and put the salsa into a bowl. Add the juice of 1 lime and ½ C. **Mexican lager**. Stir to combine. **Makes about 3 cups***

31

Breakfast & Beer
PAIRING GUIDE

BEER TYPE	FLAVOR
LAGERS	crisp, mild flavors with minimal bitterness
WHEAT BEERS	yeasty and bready flavors with smooth texture and light carbonation, sometimes with hints of citrus or other fruits
IPAs	intense bitter and hoppy flavors, often with subtle notes of citrus
AMBER ALES	strong flavors of roasted malt and sweet caramel with a crisp, dry finish
BROWN ALES	dry, nutty, and malty flavors with subtle notes of chocolate and caramel
PORTERS	roasted flavors with notes of chocolate, caramel, and coffee
STOUTS	silky texture and smooth finish with notes of chocolate and coffee

Food is better with beer, and beer is better with food... but what beer should you pair with your breakfast? Ultimately, that's up to your taste buds, but here's a handy-dandy guide to get you started. And remember, if it tastes good to you, roll with it! Everyone has different taste preferences, so don't let a beer snob shame you for drinking a lager with a donut or an IPA with a muffin. Beauty is in the eye of the beer holder.

FOODS	DESCRIPTION
 SPICY DISHES, EGGS	The crisp taste cuts through the spiciness of dishes like breakfast tacos or burritos.
 FRUITS, SWEET PASTRIES	The fruity and yeasty flavors compliment sweet breakfasts like fruit-topped waffles or jelly donuts.
 PORK, SPICY DISHES	The rich flavors in fatty or spicy foods stand up well to the bitterness of the beer.
 SPICY DISHES, EGGS	The crisp finish partners well with flavor-packed egg dishes like frittatas and eggs benedict.
 PORK, BEEF	The nutty flavors pair well with rich, hearty breakfasts like biscuits and gravy or steak and eggs.
 PORK, SWEET PASTRIES	The complex, roasted flavors pair well with rich foods like flavorful sausages or sweet pastries.
 SWEET PASTRIES , BEEF	The rich flavors in the beer pair well with rich, chocolaty pastries or flavorful, roasted meat.

Sunrise Nachos

2 T. butter
¼ C. flour
1 C. milk, divided
½ C. **lager**
¼ tsp. garlic powder
¼ tsp. salt
½ tsp. ground cumin
¼ tsp. cayenne pepper
3 C. shredded extra sharp
   cheddar cheese

4 large eggs
½ tsp.salt
1 (10 oz.) bag tortilla chips
8 slices deli ham, chopped
1 bell pepper, diced
2 green onions, sliced
½ C. salsa
Sour cream
Fresh cilantro

Directions

Melt the butter in a saucepan over medium heat and whisk in the flour. Remove the pan from the heat and whisk in ¼ cup milk until smooth. Continue adding the milk in ¼ cup increments, whisking until smooth after each addition *(it's a lot of whisking, but just consider it a morning workout)*. Stir in the beer, garlic powder, salt, cumin, and cayenne. Return the pan to the heat and stir until thick and bubbling. Remove from heat and add the cheese one handful at a time, whisking after each addition. Heat on low until you're ready to assemble the nachos.

Preheat the oven to 375°. Meanwhile, whisk together the eggs and salt. In a skillet over medium heat, scramble the eggs until set. Lay half the tortilla chips on a parchment paper lined baking sheet. Top with half of the eggs, beer cheese, ham, bell pepper, green onions, and salsa; repeat layers. Pop into the oven for 5 minutes to heat through. Top with dollops of sour cream, garnish with cilantro, and eat!

If you're looking for a quick and easy breakfast, cut up the veggies and ham the night before. You'll thank yourself in the morning!

Yes, you read that right. Nachos and beer are now part of a well-balanced breakfast. Dreams really do come true.

35

Pilsner-Battered Apple Fritters

5 T. sugar
1 T. cinnamon
2 Gala apples
2 C. flour, divided
1 C. **pilsner**
½ tsp. salt
¼ C. vegetable oil,
  plus more for frying
3 egg whites

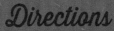

Serves 4

Directions

Mix together the sugar and cinnamon and set aside. Peel, core, and slice the apples into ½" rings. Put ½ cup flour into a dish and dredge the apple rings.

Whisk together the beer, salt, ¼ cup vegetable oil, and the remaining 1½ cups flour. Using a mixer, whip the egg whites until stiff peaks form and gently fold into the batter.

Fill a pot with 3" oil and heat to 375°. Place a wire rack over paper towels and set aside. Dip an apple ring in the batter and gently place in the oil. Cook 2 to 3 minutes on the first side, then flip and cook an additional 3 to 4 minutes. Place on the rack to cool for 1 minute. While the fritter is warm, dredge in the cinnamon-sugar mixture. Repeat for the remaining apple rings.

Say that 3 times fast (pronounced Shock-Shoo-kah)... It may be hard to say, but boy is it easy to make. This skillet dish may become your new go-to breakfast.

Chorizo Shakshuka

Preheat oven to 350°

Heat 2 T. olive oil in a cast iron skillet over medium heat. Cook 1 C. diced red potatoes and remove from skillet. In the same skillet, cook 1 sliced shallot and 1 diced bell pepper. Add 6 oz. chorizo, breaking into small pieces while cooking. Once the chorizo is almost cooked, add ½ C. **pale ale**, 1 (14 oz.) can crushed tomatoes, 1 tsp. minced garlic, ½ tsp. paprika, and ½ tsp. salt; heat for 5 minutes to reduce the sauce. Add the potatoes and stir to combine.

Make 4 wells in the mixture and crack an egg into each; bake 10 minutes. Top with cilantro, Parmesan cheese, and avocado. Serve with crusty bread to sop up the sauce.

Hey sleepyheads, this one's for you! The prep work is done the night before so you can enjoy a few extra zzz's in the morning.

Overnight Pumpkin French Toast

1 loaf Italian bread, cut into cubes

5 eggs

1 (13.5 oz.) can full-fat coconut milk

1 C. **brown ale**

1 tsp. vanilla

½ C. pumpkin purée

¼ C. brown sugar

¾ C. granulated sugar

continued next page

1½ tsp. pumpkin pie spice
½ tsp. salt
Whipped cream and
  maple syrup for serving

Directions

Put the bread cubes in an even layer in a 9 x 13″ baking dish.

In a big bowl, whisk together the eggs, coconut milk, beer, vanilla, pumpkin, brown sugar, granulated sugar, pie spice, and salt; pour evenly over the bread cubes. Cover and refrigerate overnight.

In the morning, preheat your oven to 350˚. Don't go back to bed! Walk to the fridge, take out the unbaked French toast and slide it into the oven, covered. Set the timer for 35 minutes. Now you can go back to bed. When the timer goes off, remove the cover and set the timer for 15 minutes. Take a peek in the oven; the French toast should be set and nicely browned. Top with whipped cream and syrup for serving.

Morning Michelada

*Rim a big glass with a lime wedge and dip into a mixture of 2 parts coarse salt and 1 part paprika. In the glass, mix 4 oz. vegetable juice, 2 oz. lime juice, 2 tsp. hot sauce, 1 tsp. Worcestershire sauce, and ½ tsp. fish sauce. Very slowly pour in 12 oz. **dark Mexican lager**. Add ice to fill and garnish with a lime. **Makes 1 big drink.***

Open the windows – this one's hot! Make it a little less flame-y by cutting back on the hot peppers if you must. A great eye-opener first thing in the morning.

Amber Flaming Hot Sauce

Heat 2 T. olive oil in a saucepan over medium-high heat until hot, but not smoking. In the meantime, remove the stems and seeds from 2 red bell peppers and 5 serrano chili peppers. Roughly chop the peppers, add to the hot oil, and cook for 5 minutes or until softened. Add 1 T. minced garlic and cook for 30 seconds. Slowly pour in 12 oz. **amber ale**. Stir in ½ tsp. smoked paprika, ½ tsp. salt, 1 T. rice wine vinegar, and ½ tsp. sugar and simmer for 8 minutes, stirring often. Remove the pan from the heat and let cool. Pour the sauce into a food processor and purée until smooth. Store in an airtight container in the fridge.

Use hot sauce to spice up breakfast tacos, frittatas, or anything else that needs a little kick.

This breakfast will fill you up and tickle your taste buds. You'll want to thank the pig. And the beer.

Bubbles, Spuds & Swine

2½ C. diced potatoes
¼ lb. bacon, roughly chopped
1 C. **pilsner**
1 tsp. minced garlic
½ tsp. dried parsley
Salt and black pepper to taste
About 2 T. chopped fresh dill
   (or about 2 tsp. dried)

Directions

Preheat the oven to 400° and grease a rimmed baking sheet.

Toss the potatoes and bacon into a medium bowl. Pour in the beer and stir it up really well. Dump everything out onto the prepped baking sheet and spread the potatoes in a single layer. Sprinkle with garlic, parsley, salt, and black pepper. Bake for 45 minutes, until the beer is nearly evaporated *(it seems sad, but it's ok – it's worth it).*

Remove from the oven, sprinkle with dill, and devour.

Fruit, biscuits, cream cheese, beer... all the breakfast favorites are present and accounted for in this breakfast cobbler.

Peaches & Cream Cobbler

1½ C. flour, plus more
   for dusting
¾ C. sugar, divided
1½ tsp. baking powder
¼ tsp. salt

6 T. cold butter
1 egg yolk
1 tsp. vanilla
¾ C. **cream ale**, divided
6 peaches, peeled & sliced

continued next page

½ pt. fresh blueberries
8 oz. cream cheese, cubed
¼ C. cornstarch
1 tsp. cinnamon
Zest of 1 lemon
Whipped cream for serving

Directions

Preheat the oven to 350°. In a large bowl, whisk together 1½ cups flour, ¼ cup sugar, baking powder, and salt. Grate the cold butter and stir into the mixture.

Whisk together the yolk, vanilla, and ½ cup beer. Add to the flour mixture and stir until the dough comes together. Chill while you prepare the filling.

Spread the peaches, blueberries, and cream cheese in the bottom of an 8 x 8" baking dish. Combine the remaining ½ cup sugar, cornstarch, cinnamon, zest, and the remaining ¼ cup beer in a bowl; drizzle over the fruit.

Lightly flour a surface and roll the dough into a ½"-thick circle *(adding flour as needed).* Cut the dough into rounds and place on top of the fruit. Bake for 30 to 35 minutes. Serve with a dollop of whipped cream.

Hairy Dog Mimosa
*If you're feeling fancy, grab a champagne glass for this one. Pour in about 3 oz. of pulpy orange juice and slowly add a **citrus-forward beer** to fill. That's it! Easiest cocktail ever. **Makes 1***

43

A breakfast sandwich filled with beer-doused spinach?
Popeye would be so proud.

44

Bacon, Eggs & Greens
PANINI

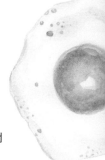

4 thick-cut bacon strips
¼ C. sliced onion
⅓ C. **brown ale**
4 C. fresh spinach
2 T. brown sugar

Pinch of red
  pepper flakes
2 eggs
Butter, softened
4 slices whole-grain bread

Directions

In a medium skillet over medium heat, cook the bacon until crisp, turning occasionally. Once crisp, transfer the bacon to paper towels; discard all but about 2 teaspoons bacon drippings from the skillet.

Add the onion to the hot drippings in the skillet and cook until caramelized, stirring occasionally. Add the beer and half the spinach; cook until slightly wilted, then add the remaining spinach. Add the brown sugar and red pepper flakes. Bring to a simmer over medium heat and cook until the beer is evaporated and the greens are tender, about 10 minutes.

Break the eggs into a clean skillet spritzed with nonstick spray. Cook over medium heat to desired doneness.

Preheat a panini press or grill pan over medium heat. Butter one side of each bread slice. Break the bacon strips in half and arrange four pieces on the unbuttered side of two of the bread slices. Top with spinach, an egg, and the remaining bread slices, butter side up. Heat until golden brown on both sides.

Pour yourself a short glass of brown ale and enjoy your sandwich.

Experiment with different types of beer for the syrup. Try one that's a bit tart, crisp, and dry. Maybe with a little funk. You should probably try several to find the one that's "just right." Do what you must.

PB & Brown Ale Waffles

1¾ C. flour
2 tsp. baking powder
1 tsp. baking soda
½ tsp. salt
2 T. cornstarch
½ C. sugar, divided

⅓ C. creamy peanut butter
¼ C. melted unsalted butter
1 C. **brown ale**
1 tsp. vanilla
2 eggs

Directions

Preheat a waffle iron.

In a big bowl, stir together the flour, baking powder, baking soda, salt, cornstarch, and ¼ cup sugar. In a small bowl, blend together the peanut butter, butter, beer, and vanilla until well blended. Separate the eggs, putting the yolks in the bowl with the peanut butter mixture and putting the whites in a separate small bowl. Stir the yolks into the peanut butter mixture until well combined. Beat the egg whites until stiff peaks form. Add the remaining ¼ cup sugar and beat until stiff peaks return.

Make a well in the dry ingredients and add the peanut butter mixture; stir until just combined. Gently fold in the egg whites.

Add batter to the waffle iron and cook according to the manufacturer's recommendation. Keep warm in a 200° oven until ready to serve. Serve with Sour Ale Cherry Syrup.

Sour Ale Cherry Syrup

*In a saucepan, combine 2 C. frozen tart cherries, 12 oz. **sour beer** (we used Berliner Weisse), and 1 C. sugar. Boil, stirring often, until thickened and the cherries have broken down. The syrup can be made several days in advance.*
Makes 3 cups

Kegs & Eggs Benny

5 egg yolks
1 C. **lager**, divided
½ C. melted butter
¼ tsp. black pepper
¼ tsp. paprika
4 eggs
2 English muffins
Arugula
4 crisp-cooked bacon strips

Directions

Whisk the yolks and ¼ cup beer in a small metal bowl; set over a pot with an inch of simmering water. Whisk the mixture until it thickens, then turn off the heat. Slowly add the butter, whisking until the mixture doubles in volume. Whisk in the black pepper and paprika. If the sauce thickens before serving, add more beer.

Fill a pot half full with water and add the remaining ¾ cup beer; bring to a gentle simmer. Break 1 egg into a bowl and slide it into the water; repeat with the remaining eggs. Lower the heat so just a few bubbles rise. Cook the eggs for about 3 minutes, until the whites set and yolks are soft; carefully remove with a slotted spoon. Split two English muffins and top each half with arugula, bacon, poached egg, and sauce.

Makes 12

Anything with fruit in it counts as a breakfast food... right? Who decides which pastries count as breakfast anyway?

Blueberry Shortcakes

Preheat the oven to 400°. Mix 4 C. biscuit baking mix, ½ C. sugar, 1 tsp. vanilla, and 12 oz. **wheat ale**. Pour into 12 greased muffin tins. Bake for 15 to 20 minutes or until a toothpick comes out clean.

For the sauce, combine 2 C. fresh blueberries, 1 C. sugar, 1 tsp. lemon zest, and 1 C. **wheat ale** in a saucepan over medium-high heat. Allow to simmer, stirring occasionally, until reduced and thickened, about 20 minutes. Spoon the sauce over the shortcakes, top with whipped cream, and enjoy!

The sauce can be made with any beer and berry combination you like. Try strawberries and lager, raspberries and pilsner, or blackberries and hefeweizen.

49

Breakfast bliss packed between two golden brown tortillas. This is the real deal. There's no turning back – you'll never look at breakfast the same way again after trying one of these bad boys.

Fajita Breakfast Quesadillas

1 lb. flat iron steak
1 bell pepper, sliced
1 small onion, sliced
12 oz. **pale ale**
1 tsp. minced garlic
½ tsp. red pepper flakes
Juice of 1 lime
¼ C. chopped fresh cilantro
1 T. olive oil

¼ tsp. ground cumin
½ tsp. paprika
½ tsp. salt
4 eggs
2 T. milk
Butter
8 (8") flour tortillas
1 C. shredded
   Pepper Jack cheese

Directions

Cut the steak into bite-sized pieces and throw into a zippered bag along with the bell pepper, onion, beer, garlic, red pepper flakes, lime juice, and cilantro; seal the bag and shake to combine. Let marinate in the fridge for 1 hour.

In a large skillet, heat oil over medium-high heat. Drain the marinade and add the steak mixture to the skillet; season with cumin, paprika, and salt. Sauté until the steak is cooked and the veggies are crisp-tender; remove from the skillet. Whisk the eggs and milk together and scramble over medium-low heat.

Heat a clean skillet over medium heat. Butter one side of a tortilla and place butter side down in the skillet. Top with some of the cheese, eggs, and steak mixture. Add another layer of cheese and top with a tortilla; butter the top tortilla before flipping. Cook until the cheese is melted. Repeat for the remaining quesadillas.

Tipsy Taters

Preheat oven to 425°. Scrub 4 russet potatoes and cut into ½" cubes. Soak the potatoes in a mixture of 12 oz. **lager**, 1 tsp. salt, and 1 tsp. minced garlic for 30 minutes, tossing halfway through. Drain the beer and toss potatoes with 2 T. olive oil, ½ tsp. salt, ½ T. seasoned salt, ½ tsp. black pepper, ½ tsp. paprika, and ¼ tsp. chili powder. Spread in a single layer on a large baking sheet lined with foil. Bake for 40 min. to 1 hour, tossing twice. **Serves 6**

Mixed Berry Sweet Rolls

3¼ C. flour, plus
  more for dusting
2 tsp. baking soda
2 tsp. baking powder
1 tsp. salt
12 oz. **wheat ale**
½ C. sugar, divided

1 C. frozen raspberries
½ C. frozen blueberries
1 tsp. cornstarch
1 C. powdered sugar
3 T. heavy cream
½ tsp. lemon zest

Directions

Preheat oven to 350°.

In a large mixing bowl, stir together 3¼ cups flour, baking soda, baking powder, salt, beer, and ¼ cup sugar until a ball of dough begins to form. Cover the dough with additional flour and transfer to a floured surface. Knead lightly until the ball forms together, adding flour as needed. Roll the dough into a large rectangle.

In a medium bowl, toss the raspberries and blueberries with the cornstarch and the remaining ¼ cup sugar. Spread the berries evenly over the dough. Tightly roll up the dough to create a log. Cut the log into 10 to 12 pieces. Place cut side up in a 9 x 13" greased baking dish. Bake for 30 to 35 minutes.

For the glaze, whisk together the powdered sugar, heavy cream, and lemon zest until smooth. Pour the glaze over the rolls and serve warm.

If you have a feeling you won't be in the baking mood in the morning, (I wonder why that could be?) make the sweet rolls up to 2 days ahead of time, cover, and refrigerate until ready to bake.

Sweet rolls without yeast... is it a miracle? Close. It's beer. The carbonation makes these rolls light and fluffy without yeast. Yet another reason to be thankful for the cold stuff.

53

Why waste your time flipping tiny pancakes all morning long when you can make one BIG pancake?

Lazy Chef's Oven Pancake

2 T. butter
⅔ C. flour
¼ C. sugar
⅓ C. **wheat ale**
⅓ C. milk
3 eggs

½ tsp. vanilla
Zest of ½ lemon
Fresh berries
Powdered sugar
Syrup

Directions

Preheat the oven to 400°. Place the butter in a 10" cast iron skillet and place in the oven to melt while the oven is preheating.

Whisk together the flour and sugar. In a separate bowl, whisk together the beer, milk, eggs, vanilla, and lemon zest. Add the wet ingredients to the dry ingredients and stir until combined. Remove the skillet from the oven and make sure the butter is distributed evenly. Pour the batter into the skillet and bake for 18 to 20 minutes or until the middle is puffed and the sides begin to curl inward *(don't worry; this baby will deflate when it's removed from the oven)*.

Top with fresh berries, powdered sugar, and a healthy dose of syrup.

Porter & PB Smoothie
*Add 2 peeled bananas, 1 C. **porter**, ¾ C. ice, ¼ C. vanilla yogurt, ¼ C. creamy peanut butter, and 2 T. unsweetened cocoa powder to a blender and process until smooth. Sip with satisfaction knowing you can feel healthy and enjoy your favorite beer – all at the same time. You're welcome. **Makes 1***

Stout Coffee Cake

2 C. granulated sugar
1¼ C. softened butter, divided
2 eggs
2 tsp. baking soda
½ tsp. salt
¼ tsp. ground nutmeg
2 tsp. cinnamon, divided
2 C. plus 2 T. **coffee stout**, divided
1 C. chopped pecans
2¼ C. flour, divided
1 C. brown sugar
½ C. old-fashioned oats
1 C. powdered sugar
1 tsp. vanilla

Directions

Preheat oven to 350°. Mix together the sugar and 1 cup butter; add the eggs, baking soda, salt, nutmeg, and 1 teaspoon cinnamon. Slowly pour in 2 cups beer while mixing; add the pecans and 2 cups flour and mix until combined. Pour the batter into a greased 9 x 13" pan.

For the crumble, combine brown sugar, oats, remaining ¼ cup flour, 1 tsp. cinnamon, and ¼ cup butter. Sprinkle half the crumble on the cake and bake at 350° for 35 to 40 minutes. Top with the remaining crumble before serving.

For the glaze, combine the powdered sugar, vanilla, and remaining 2 tablespoons beer.

The tot cups are just the vessel. Get creative and fill them with whatever you like: bacon, ham, veggies, cheese... the options are endless.

Brat & Tot Cups

Preheat the oven to 375° and grease 12 muffin tins; thaw 4 C. tater tots. Heat 2 T. olive oil in a skillet over medium heat. Add ½ C. sliced white onion, 1 T. dried parsley, and ½ lb. brats *(casings removed)*; break the brats into small pieces while cooking. Once the brats are cooked, add ½ C. **amber ale** and simmer until the beer has evaporated; drain the excess grease from the pan. Squish 4 or 5 tater tots into the bottom and sides of each muffin tin; fill each cup with the brat mixture and bake for 5 minutes.

Whisk together 6 eggs, ½ tsp salt, and ½ tsp. black pepper. Top each cup with the egg mixture and a sprinkle of cheddar cheese. Bake for 10 minutes more and enjoy!

You can't go wrong with beer bread... especially when it's packed with breakfast goodies like bacon, cheese, syrup, and jalapeños. You may want to make 2 loaves... it can't hurt to have a spare.

Kickin' Breakfast Bread

6 bacon strips
3 C. flour
1 T. baking powder
¼ tsp. salt
2 jalapeños, stems
  and seeds removed

1 C. shredded sharp cheddar
  cheese, divided
12 oz. **lager**
¼ C. maple syrup
¼ C. melted butter
2 T. brown sugar

Directions

Preheat the oven to 350°.

Crisp the bacon in a skillet. Set the bacon aside on paper towels to cool and pour the grease into a 5 x 9" loaf pan. Sift the flour, baking powder, and salt into a large mixing bowl. Roughly chop the bacon and jalapeños and add to the bowl along with ¾ cup cheddar cheese. Pour in the beer and maple syrup; stir until just combined.

Transfer the dough into the loaf pan and pour the melted butter on top *(yeah... this may not qualify as a low-calorie dish)*. Bake for 30 minutes, then sprinkle with the brown sugar and remaining ¼ cup cheddar cheese and bake for 25 minutes more. Let cool for 10 minutes before turning out of the pan.

Pour yourself a cold beer and enjoy the fruits of your labor.

Smoky Mary
*Rub the edge of a pint glass with a lemon and rim with smoked sea salt. Pour in 6 oz. tomato juice, 6 oz. **lager**, ½ oz. lemon juice, 1 tsp. barbecue sauce, ¼ tsp. chipotle powder, ¼ tsp. smoked paprika, and a dash of Worcestershire sauce. Garnish with a strip of bacon and some olives to make it a meal. **Makes 1***

Perfect on a chilly morning, this cocoa warms you up from the inside out. Add more beer if you also want to be warmed from the outside in.

A Very Stout Hot Cocoa

In a saucepan, combine 1 C. heavy cream and 3 C. whole milk; warm over medium heat until the milk is steaming but not simmering. Remove from the heat and add 6 oz. chopped bittersweet chocolate; let it sit there without disturbing it until the chocolate melts. Just hang out... Waiting...

Grab a whisk and vigorously whisk in ½ tsp. vanilla and ½ C. room-temp **oatmeal stout**, heating until the desired drinking temp. Drink immediately if you don't want to burn your taste buds. Or let it simmer until it gets as piping hot as you like it. Pour into mugs and drop in a few marshmallows.

Double, triple, or even quadruple this recipe if you're sharing. After you try this powerhouse breakfast, you'll want it again and again.

Serves 1

Traditional Muesli, But Not

⅓ C. old-fashioned oats
¼ C. **fruity beer** *(we used blueberry)*
1 Granny Smith apple
Lemon juice
⅓ C. plain Greek yogurt
½ tsp. brown sugar
Honey
Chopped walnuts
Sunflower seeds
Dried cranberries

Directions

Soak the oats in beer for 5 to 10 minutes.

Grate half the apple using the large holes of a box grater and slice the other half to use as a topping. Sprinkle some lemon juice on the apples to keep them from turning brown. Mix together the apple shreds, oats, yogurt, and brown sugar.

Cover and chill at least an hour or overnight so you can eat it the next morning. Remove from the fridge and drizzle with a little honey and top with walnuts, sunflower seeds, sliced apple, and dried cranberries.

HOO-WEE! With lots of hot chili peppers and garlic, harissa paste packs a punch. But you're having beer for breakfast, so you can handle it... right?

Zippy Morning Pizza

6 oz. pancetta

3 C. flour, plus more for sprinkling

1 T. baking powder

½ tsp. salt

12 oz. **light lager**

¼ C. harissa paste or other red chili paste

2 C. shredded mozzarella cheese

continued next page

4 eggs
2 tsp. olive oil
2 green onions, thinly sliced
Salt and black pepper to taste

Directions

Preheat oven to 450° and grease a 13" pizza pan with nonstick spray; set aside.

Toss the pancetta in a single layer on one or two baking sheets and bake about 10 minutes, until nicely browned and crispy. Move the pancetta to paper towels to drain. When cool, crumble into small pieces.

To make the dough, mix 3 cups flour, the baking powder, and the salt in a big ol' bowl. Pour in the beer and stir until combined (the dough will be sticky). Sprinkle the dough with flour so it doesn't stick to your hands; form it into a ball and use a rolling pin to roll the dough into a circle to fit in the pan. Crimp the dough to make a raised edge; poke a few holes with a fork and bake for 10 minutes. Remove from the oven, but don't turn off the heat.

Spread chili paste over the crust and top with mozzarella and the crumbled pancetta. Return to the oven and bake about 5 minutes, until the dough starts to puff and is lightly browned in a few spots.

Take the pizza out of the oven and crack the eggs on top, evenly spacing them apart; drizzle each egg with ½ teaspoon oil. Carefully put the pizza back in the oven and bake until the crust is crisp and the egg whites are set, about 10 minutes more.

Remove from the oven one last time and sprinkle with green onions, salt, and black pepper.

Index

Food

Cocktails